Published by Fox College of Business

© Bryan K. Law, 2010

All rights reserved. No part of this book may be reproduced in any form by any means, or used in any information storage and retrieval system, without the written permission of the writer.

Law, Bryan K.

Feng Shui 1 2 3

Includes index.
ISBN 978-0-9809409-3-0

1. Feng Shui   2. Geomancy – Canada

Printed in Canada

Disclaimer

Fox College of Business, Bryan K. Law and every person involved in the creation of this book, disclaim any warranty as to the accuracy, completeness and currency of the contents of this book.

The adoption and application of the advice and information offered are solely the readers' responsibilities. We make no claim for absolute effectiveness and we disclaim all liability in respect of the results of any action taken or not taken in reliance upon information in this book.

Errata Sheet

P. 112

For example, a house with a missing corner at the <u>east</u> means the eldest son will have bad luck. If the family has no son, it will mean the couple will not have son but daughters.

P.114 The diagram should be

South East	South	South West
<u>Eldest Daughter</u>	<u>Middle Daughter</u>	<u>Mother</u>
East <u>Eldest Son</u>		West <u>Youngest Daughter</u>
North East <u>Youngest Son</u>	North <u>Middle Son</u>	North West <u>Father</u>

This book is dedicated to my wife,

*Gladys, my confidante and best friend,
for her thoughtfulness and continuing support;*

and to our daughters:

*Tania,
for her unique artistic talents and sensitivity; and*

*Evelyn,
for her wonderful sense of humour and creativity.*

This book is also dedicated to my late father,

Simon, for his selfless and endless love.

Bryan K. Law, BSc, LLM

Bryan's background is deeply real estate related; author, broker, consultant, Feng Shui consultant, instructor and lease auditor – he is widely regarded as one of the foremost real estate instructors in Canada.

After 20 years of study, Bryan started giving Feng Shui advice to his real estate clients. After a few years as an amateur Feng Shui consultant, Bryan found that many people still had many wrong interpretations and misunderstandings in Feng Shui. As a result, he decided to educate the public what Feng Shui is in a website, as well as to teach people the basic knowledge in Feng Shui by delivering some Feng Shui courses.

Author of the best selling investment book *"Real Estate; Every One Can Afford It!"*, numerous articles in journals, newsletters and newspapers.

Bryan K. Law BSc, LLM
FRI, CLO, CLA, REI, RPA, MVA – Residential
www.bedroomfengshuitips.com

Table of Contents

Preface   P.1

Introduction   P.5

Section I – The Basics   P.17

Section II – Exterior Feng Shui   P.35

Section III – Interior Feng Shui   P.74

Appendix   P.131

Preface

About This Book

This book was written with two groups of readers in mind. Whether you are new to Feng Shui and want to learn it, or already know the concept of it but want to find out more about how to handle the common challenges, we hope that you will find what follows both instructive and entertaining too.

This is not an introduction to Feng Shui theories, or a detailed explanation of different streams and schools in Feng Shui practice. Instead, the purpose of this book is to point out the common Feng Shui challenges found in most real properties and suggest solutions to those challenges.

Approach Used

There were two main streams in the development of Feng Shui, one relied mainly on geography without using a compass (Form stream) and the other one relied on compass and figures (Compass stream).

Form stream came from the natural instincts of the Chinese ancestors who looked for the best place to reside by studying the geography of the area, such as topography and climate. It has to consider a wide range of area, normally within what our bare eyes can see.

Compass stream uses a compass to determine the direction is good or not, with the addition of other methods and theories, such as Bagua and Flying Stars. It has to consider the time, mainly the year, when Feng Shui is applied.

These two streams are interwoven and modern Feng Shui consultants will often use the methods from both streams to achieve the best results. As our societies are better developed and regulated than in the ancient times, it is impossible to build a home or a graveyard anywhere as we wish. We have to build houses on residential zoned lands and bury the deceased only in a licensed graveyard. Since our societies are more micro-managing the use of land, it makes the land use more inflexible and Feng Shui consulting is frequently limited to the micro level.

As Feng Shui was originally developed for choosing places for burial sites, its theories changed accordingly when it was applied to homes. However, many people overlook this point and apply the techniques in finding good graveyards directly to homes, which is very dangerous.

Although the methods we use are based on the both streams in Feng Shui study, we put more emphasis on the Form stream as it is independent to one's birthday (the trigram).

This kind of approach can make sure that the solutions which are the best remedies for you are basically generic in nature.

To draw an analogy, the challenges mentioned in this book are like junk foods and bad habits that weaken your health and should be avoided. The remedies used in this book are like common health foods and simple exercises to improve your health, regardless of your gender and age.

If you are sick, you need to see a doctor. Medicine will be given according to your personal needs. Similarly, for a detailed improvement of your Feng Shui, it is necessary to consult a Feng Shui practitioner.

Because of the reasons above, this book is better for beginners than professional Feng Shui advocates.

Introduction

What is Feng Shui?

Feng Shui is the Chinese term for geomancy; a system of aesthetics with well developed theories, using geographic features, figures, directions, and the laws of nature to help one improve life by balancing the five elements - Earth, Metal, Water, Wood and Fire. Its theories rely on both Heaven (astronomy) and Earth (geography) that cover everything human beings have to deal with, both tangibly and intangibly.

Feng Shui means Wind and Water in Chinese. Its meaning emphasizes the importance of flow of Qi - both tangible and intangible. Wind can mean wind, rain, snow, sunlight, sound, magnetic fields, electromagnetic fields, infrared lights, radon gas, etc and Water can mean rivers, creeks, roads, flows of traffic and etc; they can also mean other tangible and intangible things that may not be known by us. For example, people did not know anything about radioactive substances, invisible lights and ultra high frequency sound waves one thousand years ago; but these substances did exist at that time. Feng Shui is a study on how the environment would affect people, by statistics and theories that have been developed for over four thousand years.

The Success of Feng Shui

Feng Shui is an ancient Chinese tradition with thousand years of history. There are countless examples of both successes and failures. People would, however, be skeptical that Feng Shui does not work in the western world, or even not work outside of China. There are, fortunately, many people who experienced the effect of Feng Shui and can tell you their successful stories. Ask the people around you and there will be some cases to share.

A lady told a group of people that her cousin was diagnosed with terminal cancer. One day her Chinese friend visited her cousin and told her that there was a severe Feng Shui problem in the cousin's house which had to be corrected. The cousin just corrected it by moving some furniture. Miraculously, the tumour disappeared when the cousin had the ultra-sound scan done a month later.

This was one of the miracles that happened around us, but was effective enough to show the power of Feng Shui.

How Much Can Feng Shui Help You?

First of all, let us draw an analogy. Feng Shui to a property is like a garment to a person. You have to choose suitable clothes according to your profession. If you are a businessman, you will need a suit; if you are an athlete, you will need a sport suit; if you are a diver, you will need a diving suit; etc and etc. Wearing inappropriate garment may hinder your performance, risk your career and even risk your life.

On the other hand, wearing an appropriate garment does not guarantee your success. If you are not a top athlete, wearing a sport suit will not make you a champion. However, it will not hinder your performance and will lower down your risk in injury. In other words, wearing an appropriate garment can maximize your performance and give you the biggest protection.

Feng Shui has the same functions to properties. Having a good Feng Shui can boost your luck; you will be able to maximize your return. However, it is not a guarantee of success; for example, you cannot just sit and wait for your luck to come without doing anything.

Can Feng Shui Bring Bad Luck?

Definitely! You may have good Feng Shui and can have bad Feng Shui too. Having bad Feng Shui is like eating poisoned foods which can bring you sickness or even death.

Some Feng Shui practitioners like to use special settings of Feng Shui in order to maximize the effects. Such settings require complex and accurate calculations of one's trigram, directions and flying stars. Since there is a high risk, only people with challenging goals will take such risk. Ordinary people should not take such an approach as the risk is too high and it may not be worth to take it.

Moreover, Feng Shui relies on the universe, and righteousness is a foundation of it. One cannot use Feng Shui to assist illegal activities or to cover them. A famous Feng Shui master was hired by an accused to assist him in defending the prosecution by putting up a special Feng Shui setting; however the accused was eventually convicted as there were tons of evidences to prove his participation in that illegal activity. This is an example to show Feng Shui does not help people in that way.

Contemporary Feng Shui

It is undeniable that Feng Shui is an ancient subject. As society has developed and people have evolved, it is necessary to make Feng Shui practices adapt to our new society. For example, there was no electric tower, no flyover and no subway one hundred years ago; but we have to deal with these Feng Shui problems now. This is how the term *Contemporary Feng Shui* comes.

The fact is: our society did not change overnight. Feng Shui has been developed, expanded, modified and improved to fit the changes of society in the past four thousand years. It keeps on changing everyday and it is contemporary already. If you study the Feng Shui nowadays and compare with those in the ancient books, you will find that many theories have already been added to it. The principles, however, are still the same.

Some geomancers copied some theories from Feng Shui without knowing its principles, added their own stuff to it and called it *contemporary Feng Shui*. That is unacceptable. Some geomancers said it was not good to place a single lamp post in front of a bed, as it meant 'One Night Stand'; which was not good for getting or maintaining a stable relationship.

They simply used the 'homophonic' words – 'One Light Stand' to 'One Night Stand'. Many people would find this funny and accept the interpretation of it. It is not sure if such kind of geomancy works or not, but definitely it is not Feng Shui.

Did the Chinese speak English four thousand years ago as their mother tongue? Did the term 'One Night Stand' appear four thousand years ago? Definitely not! There is no way such kind of geomancy to be part of Feng Shui.

You may copy a Chinese character, use it as a pattern, and write it in different fonts. You can even change the character into a diagram in a way that the diagram is no longer a Chinese character. People may admire this as a fine art. However, you cannot use such diagrams to write a Chinese essay. No one in the world will be able to understand such essay except you. It is because the 'characters' you used are no longer Chinese characters; they are just some 'diagrams' invented by you.

The same logic applies to some of the so-called contemporary Feng Shui promoters. Feng Shui is not a fine art and cannot be changed that way. Those promoters just used a small portion of Feng Shui concepts and called their new inventions 'contemporary Feng Shui'.

Contemporary Feng Shui is not a phrase used to twist the meaning of Feng Shui; it should be genuine Feng Shui with modern applications.

To be fair to everyone - the genuine Feng Shui practitioners, believers and general public, those contemporary Feng Shui without the support of full Feng Shui principles should not be called Feng Shui. They should be called Geomancy Design, or Contemporary Geomancy, or any other name, but NOT Feng Shui.

Section I – The Basics

Before you can set a better Feng Shui for your home, there is some basic knowledge that you need to know.

Loupan

A Feng Shui consultant who uses Bagua to tell Feng Shui must also use Loupan (Figure 1) to tell the directions. Otherwise, it is like using a map to find roads in the wild without the assistance of a compass.

Unfortunately, there are many 'Feng Shui' practitioners using Bagua to tell Feng Shui without using Loupan, saying that those are 'contemporary' Feng Shui.

That kind of 'Feng Shui' will not be accurate and, even worse; it may bring opposite or harmful effects to the people who set their properties according to those types of theories.

Loupan is actually a compass with two lines and a rotatable table. The two lines are perpendicular to each other with the intersection at the centre of the compass.

The rotatable table is in fact a 'cheat sheet' that contains all the directions, names, readings, and all other information for applying Bagua.

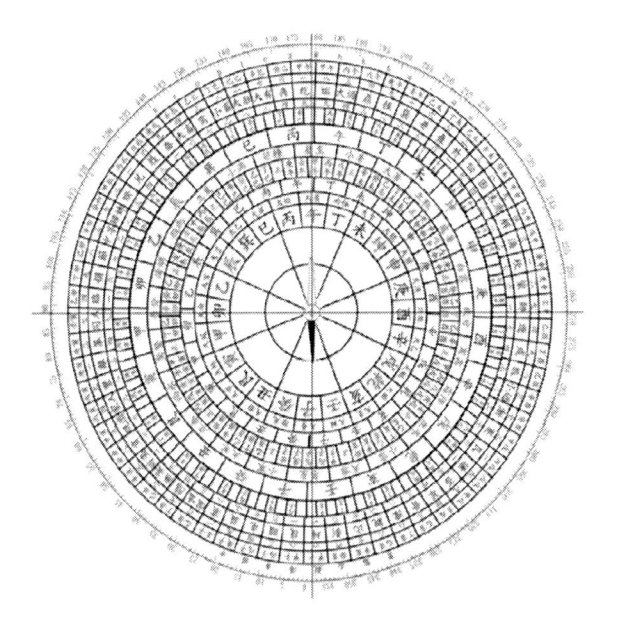

Figure 1

Loupan – Chinese compass used in Feng Shui.

Qi

Qi (or Chi) is frequently translated as "energy flow". It is a concept of circulation or movement of some tangible or intangible materials. There is Qi in the universe, in the sky, on the earth, inside our homes and even inside our bodies.

Qi can be good or bad; wind, light, infrared, radioactive substances, invisible lights, and ultra high frequency sound waves can all be Qi. In Feng Shui, we want to block the bad Qi or aggressive Qi; and to welcome good Qi and have a good circulation of Qi.

Yin and Yang

Yin Yang is a Chinese philosophy. Yin and Yang are two contrary forces (or fields) that are interconnected and interdependent in the natural world, and they give rise to each other in turn.

When the Yang dominates and eventually takes over the whole environment (100%), it will reduce its power and the Yin will overcome Yang and start another cycle. However, the time length for each cycle is unknown and may not be equal.

For example, if fire is Yang and water is Yin, a piece of burning charcoal will consume all its contents (including water molecules inside) and become ashes. When the fire extinguishes, the Yang is gone and the ashes starts to absorb moisture in the atmosphere and the Yin takes back the control.

Chinese philosophy believes Yin and Yang are always paired and have to be balanced.

Examples

Yin	Yang
Female	Male
Earth	Sky
North	South
Wet	Dry
Dark	Bright
Cold	Hot

How to Balance Yin Yang

Yin and Yang has to be balanced. For example, when the house is too cold, we have to turn on the furnace to warm it up; when it is too hot, we have to turn on the air conditioning unit to cool it down.

When a house is too wet, you need a dehumidifier to take away the moisture. When your home is too dry, you need a humidifier to give some moisture to it.

When a house is too bright, such as a sun drenched California kitchen, you need some blinds to block the sun. When a room does not have enough light, you should consider adding a more powerful electric light fixture or simply change the light bulb if possible.

A noisy home is disturbing; you need good quality windows to eliminate the exterior noise or turn down the volume of your audio and video system.

The colours have to be balanced too, not too bright and not too dark. A room that is too bright will make people active all the time; while a room that is too dark will make people bored and lazy.

All of the above are the examples of balancing Yin and Yang.

The Five Elements

The concept of Five Elements has been used in many traditional Chinese fields, such as astrology, traditional Chinese medicine, music, military strategy and martial arts. Its general meaning is Five Movements or Five Phases.

Five movements are centre (earth), right (metal), left (wood), forward (fire) and backward (water). Five phases are sink (metal), wet (water), grow (wood), hold (earth), heat (fire).

In Feng Shui, it also represents the natures of directions and the Flying Stars.

The five elements are interrelated and there are two basic cycles – the controlling cycle and the nurturing cycle (Figure 2).

While a Feng Shui consultant will use as many as four cycles and eight scenarios to balance the elements; these two basic cycles explain the main theories of Five Elements.

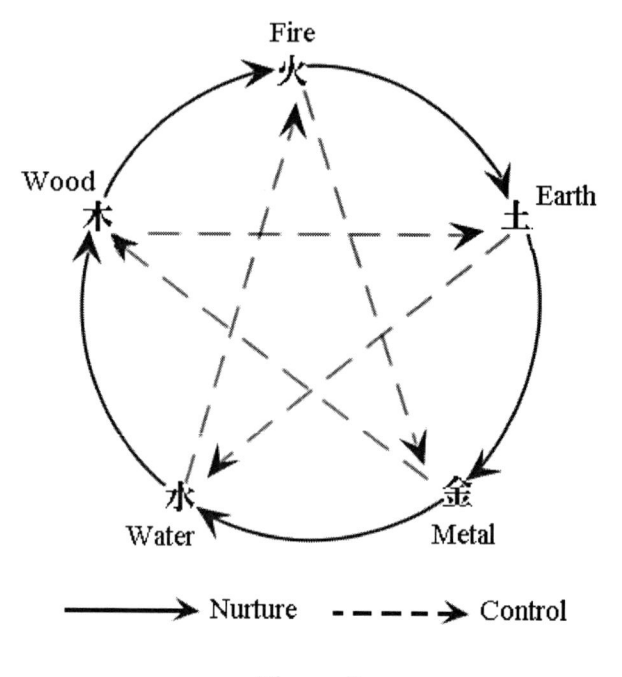

Figure 2

The two basic cycles of five elements

The controlling cycle is explained by: Fire melts Metal, Metal pierces Wood, Wood burdens Earth, Earth absorbs Water and Water extinguishes Fire.

The nurturing cycle is explained by: Fire makes Earth, Earth produces Metal, Metal enriches Water, Water feeds Wood and Wood fuels Fire.

Whenever one element is too weak or we want to boost that element, we may increase it by providing the same element or by adding more its nurturing element.

On the contrary, when we want to reduce or control one element, we should avoid using such an element and should introduce its controlling element to the property.

Bagua

Bagua is a diagram that consists of eight small diagrams to represent the fundamental principles of reality, seen as a range of eight interrelated concepts. Each consists of three lines, each line either "broken" or "unbroken," representing yin or yang, respectively. It is also used to represent the directions.

There are two versions of Bagua, Earlier Heaven Bagua (Figure 3) and Later Heaven Bagua (Figure 4).

The Earlier Heaven Bagua was used in China in around 172 BCE. It was used as a tool to study many fields. The numbers 1 to 9 were assigned to the nine different part of a 3x3 square.

The way that the numbers assigned was actually the Magic Square as found in a mathematics problem (Figure 5). Such discovery was about 1,800 years earlier than Claude Gaspar Bachet's work (1581 –

1638, a French mathematician who found a method of constructing magic squares).

The Compass stream uses Bagua in studying and applying Feng Shui. Some 'schools' propose that every home should be divided into nine equal portions. Each portion is assigned to control the luck of different aspects (Figure 6).

Figure 3

Earlier Heaven Bagua

Figure 4

Later Heaven Bagua

4	9	2
3	5	7
8	1	6

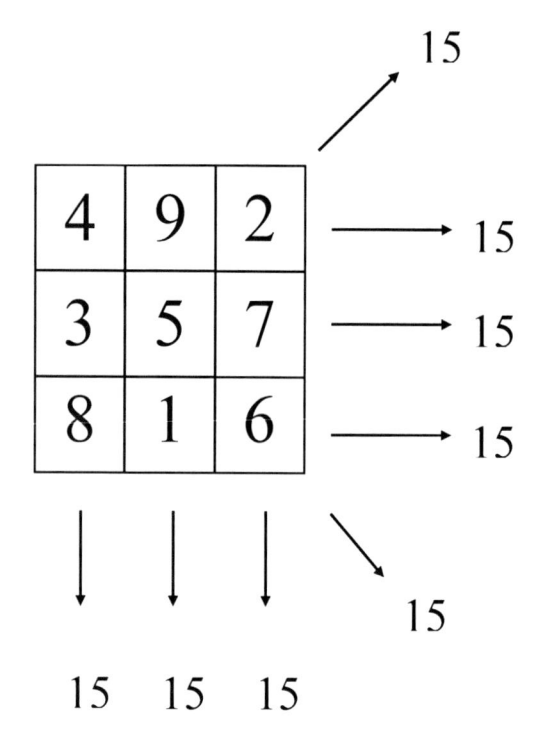

Figure 5

A Magic Square with the sum of horizontal, vertical, and diagonal numbers all equal to 15.

Career **North** (Water)	Knowledge & Wisdom **North East** (Earth)	Health & Family **East** (Wood)
Helps & Friends **North West** (Metal)	**Centre** (Earth)	Wealth **South East** (Wood)
Children & Creativity **West** (Metal)	Love & Marriage **South West** (Earth)	Fame & Reputation **South** (Fire)

Figure 6

A sample sheet that used by Compass stream.

Sha

Sha is the Chinese name for 'evil'. Sha is generated by blocked Qi, aggressive Qi, destructive Qi, unbalanced Yin and Yang or an unbalanced force from the five elements.

Whenever there is a Sha, we have to break it down, divert it, block it, or absorb it; so that it will not hurt you.

The main purpose of this book is to tell you what the common Sha are, and the methods to overcome them.

Section II – Exterior Feng Shui

It does not matter if you are living in a detached house or in an apartment unit, the exterior Feng Shui of your home will affect you the same way as the interior Feng Shui does. Therefore, it is important to know the characteristics of your neighbourhood in order to improve your Feng Shui.

Most of the exterior Feng Shui are out of your control. For example, you cannot change the shape of the hill or the height of buildings around you; you cannot demolish a flyway or a hydro tower nearby and you cannot change the direction of road or the location of buildings.

However, there are methods to solve the exterior Feng Shui problems from the interior or exterior settings of your home.

Bad Odour

Bad odour is a kind of Sha in Feng Shui, which brings bad luck to the residents. Bad odour is harmful to you not only physically and psychologically, but also to your luck.

It is one of the tangible Sha in Feng Shui and also one of the worst. If you notice bad odour coming from the outside of your property, you should find out the source and eliminate such odour.

Bad odour may come from decayed leaves and barks that have fallen from trees, still water, animal feces, or industrial facilities nearby. If the odour comes from your own land, you should solve the problems immediately by cleaning the land and cutting off the source.

If the odour is from other sites, you should find out the source and report it to the corresponding authority so that it can be stopped as soon as possible.

Branches of Tree Pointing Your Home

If you live in a house or a unit in an apartment on the lower levels, you should pay attention to those trees that are close to your home. When the tree branches are pointing towards your home, it is a Sha. The closer the branches, the worse the Sha is (especially when they are pointing towards your bedroom).

If the branches are pointing towards the windows, the Sha will cause discomfort or illness to your eyes. If the tree is so close that the branches or leaves reach your exterior wall or window pane, immediate action is needed.

You should trim the tree to terminate the Sha. If the tree belongs to someone else or it is a public property so that you cannot trim it, you can place a dry calabash (or calabash shape ornament, Figure 7) on the interior of the wall that is facing the tree. A piece of jade will also serve the purpose.

For windows, in addition to the methods above, you should keep the blinds closed if the tree cannot be trimmed.

Figure 7

A Calabash

Chimney Nearby

A tall chimney is a type of Sha (Figure 8); especially the big stand alone chimneys used in heavy industries, power generation plants, and incinerators.

The shape of a chimney is a tall pole, representing Wood. The physical nature of a chimney is extremely hot, representing Fire.

Putting these two characteristics together would mean a large burning wood, which is extremely Fire. If you can see such a chimney from the outside or inside of your home, then the Sha will affect you.

The best way to deal with this kind of Sha is to reduce its power. You can put a large stone statute outside your door, or in front of the exterior wall that faces the chimney to absorb the Sha. As stone is Earth, the Fire from the Chimney will be absorbed by Earth.

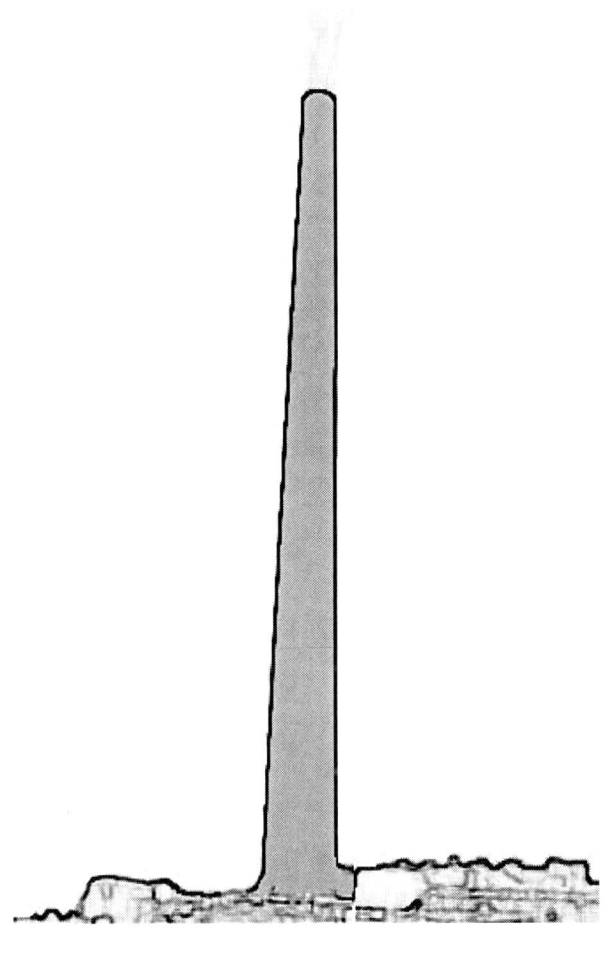

Figure 8

A Chimney is like a large piece of burning log, which is a strong Sha

If you belong to Water, and the Sha is NOT from the west or north-west side; you can put a metal item (such as a stand) with the stone statue. The logic is: Fire nurtures Earth, Earth nurtures Metal, and Metal nurtures Water.

Curved Road

Buildings sitting opposite to a curved road are facing an Anti-Bow Sha (Figure 9), which is not good. On the contrary, if the building is sitting on the interior side of the curved road (Figure 10), it is good. The building is like being protected by an arm; and the Qi will arrive calmly.

For a building that is sitting opposite to a curved road, the Qi will be too strong and the building is like being but by a saber (the anti-bow shaped road).

The worst situation of a curved road is when there is a streetlight pole or a tree on it (Figure 11). For all cases, you can plant some dwarf spruce trees (nine trees recommended, cone and round shapes alternatively, planted in an L shape or curve shape) in the front yard to guard the entrance, or you can plant nine small bamboos inside, in a round shape and place them facing the curved road.

Figure 9

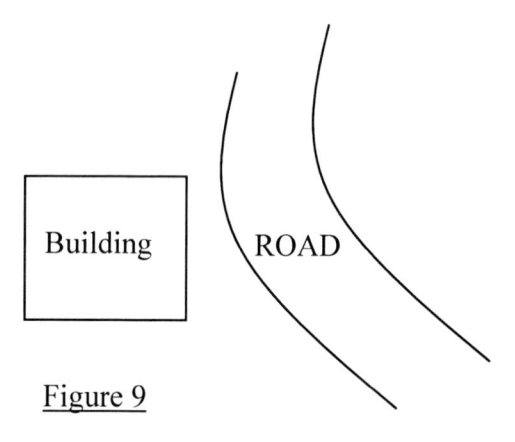

A building on the opposite side of a curved road is not good.

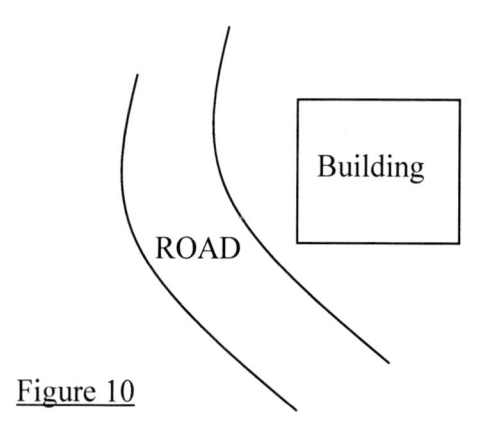

Figure 10

A building on the interior of a curved road is good.

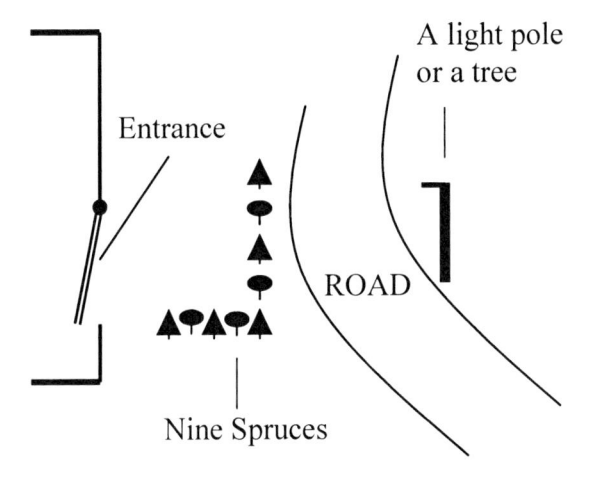

Figure 11

The streetlight pole is like an arrow on a bow, shooting the building.

45

Dying Trees

Dying trees or withering branches represent fading and failing. If they are on the left hand side of your building (when you face the road outside), the Sha will harm the male master more. If they are on the right hand side, the Sha affects the female master. If they are at the back of the house, it means the masters will have a lack of support from their bosses or friends. Dying trees should be cut down and withering branches should be trimmed immediately to prevent the Sha from functioning.

Again, if the tree belongs to someone else or it is a public property so that you cannot trim it, you can place a dry calabash (or calabash shape ornament) on the interior of the wall that is facing the tree. A piece of jade can also serve the purpose. For windows, in addition to the methods above, you should keep the blinds closed if the tree cannot be trimmed.

Elevator

If you live in a high-rise building and the door of your unit is directly facing an elevator door, it will make you lose money and cause bad health.

You can put a concave mirror above your unit door, facing the inside. This can prevent the good Qi of your home from leaving. A dry calabash or its statute can be placed on a spot that faces directly to the door to absorb the bad Qi from the elevator (Figure 12).

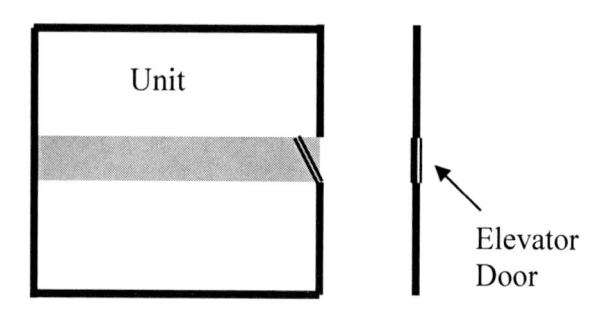

Figure 12

The calabash can be placed anywhere on the shaded area.

Extended Upper Level

Some houses have extended upper levels and some buildings are also built in the shape as a flag (Figure 13). Such a shape is like standing with one foot, which is unstable and unsafe.

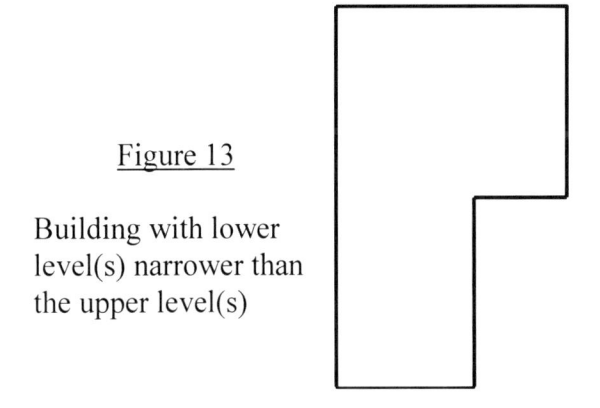

Figure 13

Building with lower level(s) narrower than the upper level(s)

If you see such a kind of building, the best idea will be to not move in. If you are already living there, the remedy will be to put an elephant statute to a good spot as a support. The best spot can be found by a Feng Shui practitioner, but the middle part of the back of your home (Figure 14) is always one of the good spots you can use.

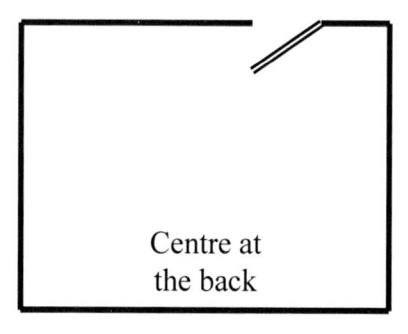

Centre at
the back

Figure 14

Facing a Sharp Edge

Sharp branches of a tree pointing to your home are not good, nor are the sharp edges of other buildings nearby (Figure 15). They produce Sha that point to your home.

The edge of another building is a Sha; it is like a knife pointing to you. If it is far away, the effect will not be significant. If it is very close, such as two high-rise buildings close to each other, the Sha will be very strong.

To block such kind of Sha, you can keep the blinds of windows on that side closed. You can also place a piece of jade on that side of wall if there is no window. If there is a window but you are not willing to keep the blinds closed, you can hang a dry calabash or its statute on that window (or place it on the window sill).

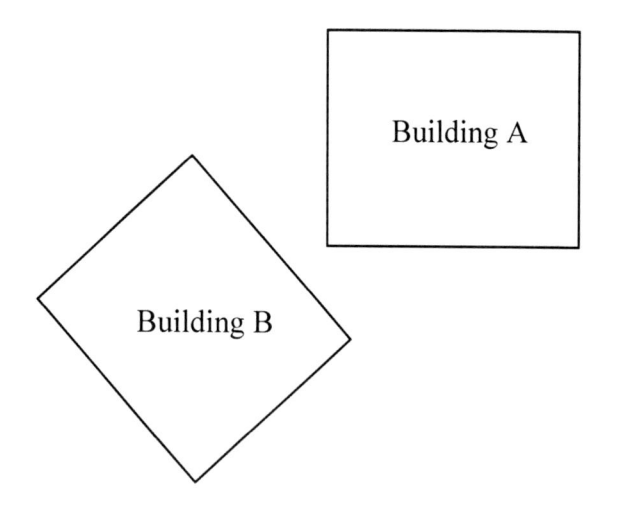

Figure 15

Building B is facing the sharp point of Building A. People who live in that side of Building B are facing a Sha.

Front Door Facing a Tree or a Pole

If there is a tree or a pole directly in line with your front door, then it is like a piece of fish bone stabbing into your throat or a spear pointing to your heart.

If it is a tree, the simplest way will be to cut it down. However, you have to make sure there is no other Sha behind that tree. Otherwise, cutting down that tree will expose you to another Sha, which may be even stronger.

If the tree cannot be cut down or it is a utility pole, then you can put a turtle statute on the outside, as close to your front door as possible. Placing some plants outside on the side facing the tree or pole is also an alternative.

If you have an exterior light on the side that is facing the pole, you can keep it on all the time. You can also place a red triangle made with plastic material to face to the pole.

Front Door Directly Facing a Road

If the front door of a house is directly facing a road (Figure 16), the best idea will be to not buy it.

If, however, you are already living in such a house, you can plant nine spruces in the front yard to guard your house (Figure 11).

You can also relocate your entrance door from the spot facing the road to the other part of the wall; or simply use the side door or back door (if there is one) and keep the front door locked.

You can also place a screen behind your front door to block the aggressive Qi from the road if your foyer is big enough to accommodate that (Figure 17).

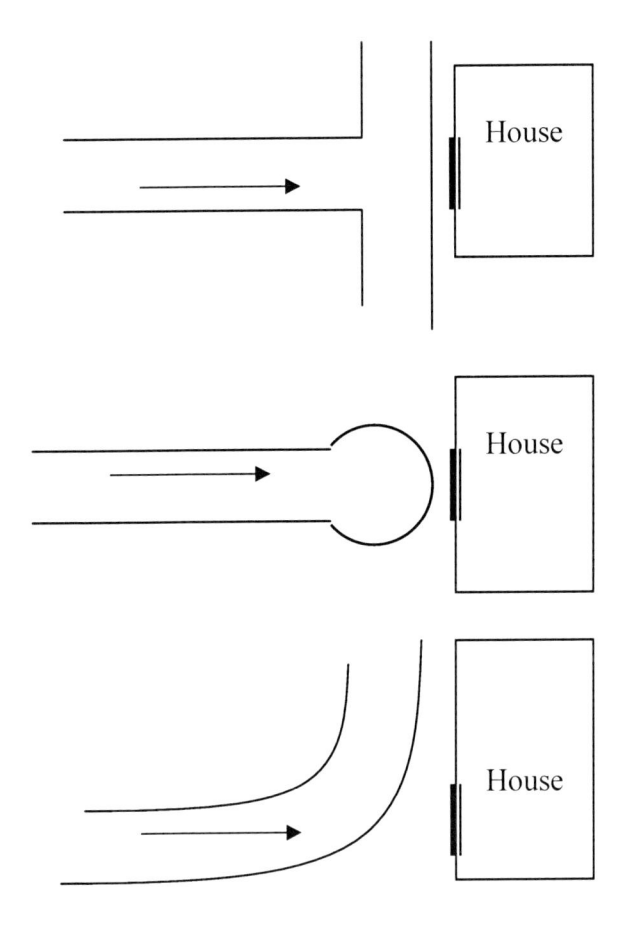

Figure 16

All the houses above are directly facing a road.

55

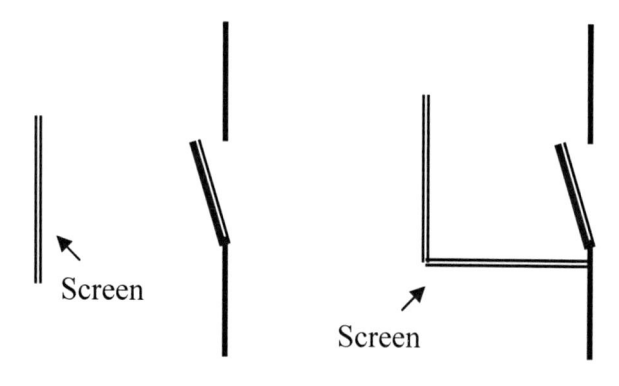

Figure 17

Screens can be set behind the door, as shown above

Light and Water Reflection

Light that is too strong or from an improper source is also a Sha. There are glass buildings that may reflect sunlight to your home, or a pool of water in your yard that may reflect the sunlight to your ceiling, or other things that may reflect or refract sunlight into your home. All these lights should be eliminated or blocked.

A pool of water can be cleaned up as soon as you wish; but if it is a swimming pool, then you have to use another method to deal with it.

The blinds of the window that the light is coming through should be kept closed. If the blinds cannot be kept closed, then you can put a big plant or some small plants near that window to block some of the light. The big plant should be foliage plants and small ones can be little bamboos.

Light that is reflected and refracted by crystal balls is also a kind of Sha, which makes people dizzy. Some geomancers advise people to use crystals to refract light as a kind of Qi. You should know that those crystal balls are artificial crystals which did not exist in ancient time. More importantly, such kind of light is a Sha. This kind of method is simply not a Feng Shui tool.

Some Feng Shui consultants do use natural crystals as tools, but they do not use them to refract light. Natural crystal balls are used to reflect bad Qi by their convex surface, similar to the effect of turtle statutes.

If you have hung such kind of artificial crystal balls in your home or inside your car, you should take them down.

Location of Building

You should always pay attention to the surroundings of the property before buying it. It is better to buy a home with safe and sound Feng Shui without worrying how to rectify the problems than buying a house with Feng Shui challenges and getting the best solutions to fix them.

Having said that, it is unlikely you can find a home with perfect Feng Shui. While you can renovate the interior of your home, the surrounding environment is out of your control. It is therefore crucial to check the surrounding area before buying a home. If your home is close to a hospital, graveyard or funeral home, there will be too much Yin in your area and you will have to boost up the Yang in your home.

You can put a dry calabash or its statute on a good spot. Again, the best spot can be found out by a Feng Shui consultant, but you can always put it in the middle part of the back of your home (Figure 14).

If possible, you can also keep a light on all the time to enhance the Yang in your home.

Ocean Views and Lake Views

Homes with magnificent ocean views or lake views are always welcome, especially for million dollar homes. They are, however, not necessarily good Feng Shui homes to us.

If the view is a small lake or part of the sea with hills beyond the water (Figure 18), it is a very good Feng Shui.

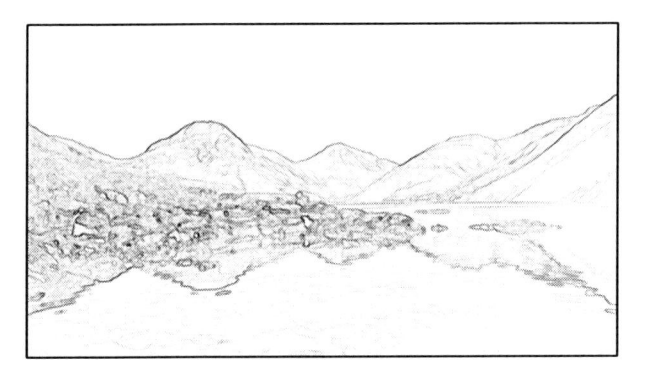

Figure 18

An ocean view (lake view) with boundaries

Since water represents wealth and there is abundance of water in the sea (lake); that means it is a wealthy home. If the water is trapped by the hills; that will mean you can retain your wealth.

On the contrary, if the view is facing an open ocean or open lake (Figure 19), the water is too vigorous and is not good in Feng Shui. The Qi is simply too strong; and when the waves hit the shores, the strong Qi attacks you. When the water recedes back to the ocean (lake), it will bring away your luck and wealth.

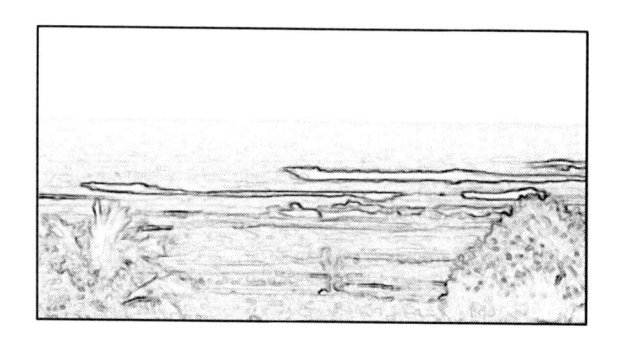

Figure 19

A view facing an open ocean (open lake)

You can block the top of the view by lowering down your horizontal blinds and placing some foliage plants in clay pots to block the view. Plants are Wood, so they can weaken the Water from the sea. Clay pots are Earth in nature, can absorb the Water from the sea.

If you are living in a house, you can plant some trees in the yard between the sea and your house so that the open ocean will not directly affect your house.

If there is an island in the centre of the water but there are open waters on the sides (Figure 20), the waters in both sides will still bring your luck away. You can use vertical blinds to block the two sides and put plants to block the Qi in the same ways that were shown as above.

Figure 20

An island in the middle part of the view

Rocky Hills or Bald Slopes

Rocky hills represent ominousness and bald slopes represent decadence. They are not good Feng Shui, especially when they are at the back of your home.

You can put a dry calabash or its statute on a good spot. Again, the best spot can be found out by a Feng Shui consultant, but you can always put it in the middle part of the back of your home (Figure 14).

If the rocky hill or bald slope is at the back of your home, you should keep the blinds at the back closed. You can place an elephant statute to the middle part of the back of your home instead of a calabash.

Stand Alone High-rise Building

We have many high-rise buildings in downtown areas nowadays; but in some areas, there may be only one high-rise building in that neighbourhood (Figure 21).

A stand alone high-rise building creates a Lonely Sha; people living inside this kind of building will end up having a lonely life. Either the residents will be single for life, or their children will leave them and seldom visit them, or they will simply have no friends.

To solve this kind of Sha, you can hang a piece of jade or place a dry calabash (or a calabash shape ornament) to the wall of a good spot. Again, the best spot can be found by a Feng Shui practitioner, but the middle part of the back of your home (Figure 14) is always one of the good spots you can use.

One thing that must be mentioned is that all people who can see such a building in their homes will also be affected the Sha.

If you can see such a single high-rise building from your home, you can put the jade or calabash to the wall that is closest to that building to absorb the Sha.

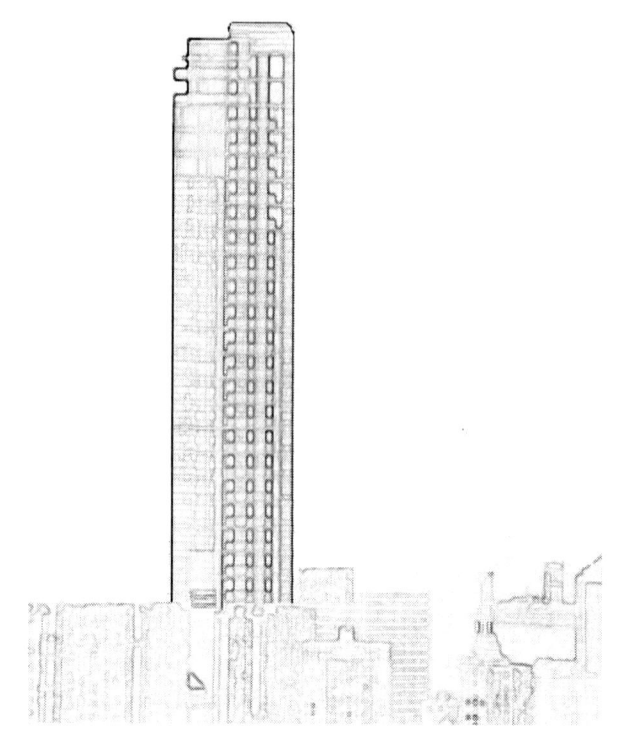

Figure 21

Stand alone high-rise buildings cause loneliness

Stone Walkway

Stone walkways, especially those with large stepping stones (Figure 22), are beautiful and give the site a natural look. However, they are not good.

Stone walkway is not only bad in Feng Shui; it is not safe when it is uneven. In Feng Shui, it represents difficulties and hurdles; thus it should be avoided.

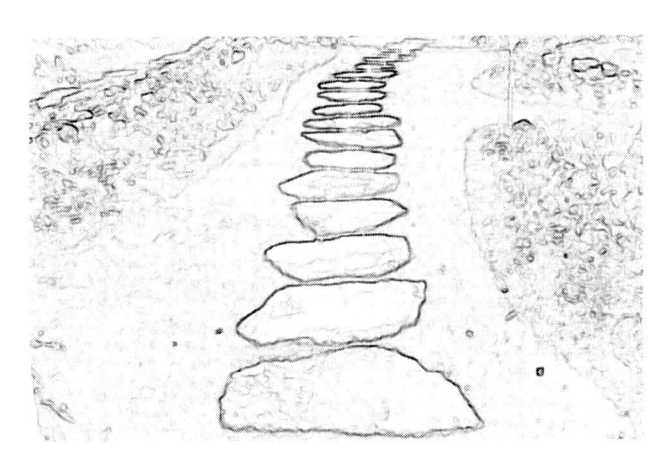

Figure 22

An uneven stone walkway

If you do have such kind of stone walkway in your yard, you should either remove the stones or make the road flat by putting some gravel and sand around the stones to replace the lawn.

Subway Tunnel Underneath

It was inconceivable that in ancient time that there would be a tunnel underneath your home that might run for miles. There were, however, hollow grounds and underground creeks that would weaken the foundation of houses.

Modern technology can strengthen the foundations of buildings so that subway tunnels can pass through the underground of high-rise buildings without worrying about affecting the foundations. However, the Sha in Feng Shui is still there since it is a hollow shape underneath a home.

You can put an elephant statute to the middle part of the back of your home (Figure 14) as a support and put a piece of jade in a good spot. Although only Feng Shui practitioners can find the best spot, you can place the jade to the same spot as the elephant. A large jade elephant can serve both purposes.

Two Buildings That Are Too Close

When two multi-level buildings are built too closely, they create an Axed Sha (Figure 23). In ancient time, such kind of Sha would not be strong as the buildings were not high. Now, we have the skyscrapers in many cities and some of them are twin buildings. These create very strong Axed Sha.

When two skyscrapers are closely built, the Axed Sha is strong and the damage can be very significant.

For buildings with strong Axed Sha, it does not matter if it is an apartment or an office building; the best idea is not to move in.

If you have to live or work inside, you can put a piece of jade on the wall that is facing the other building, or on the wall that is closest to the gap between the two buildings.

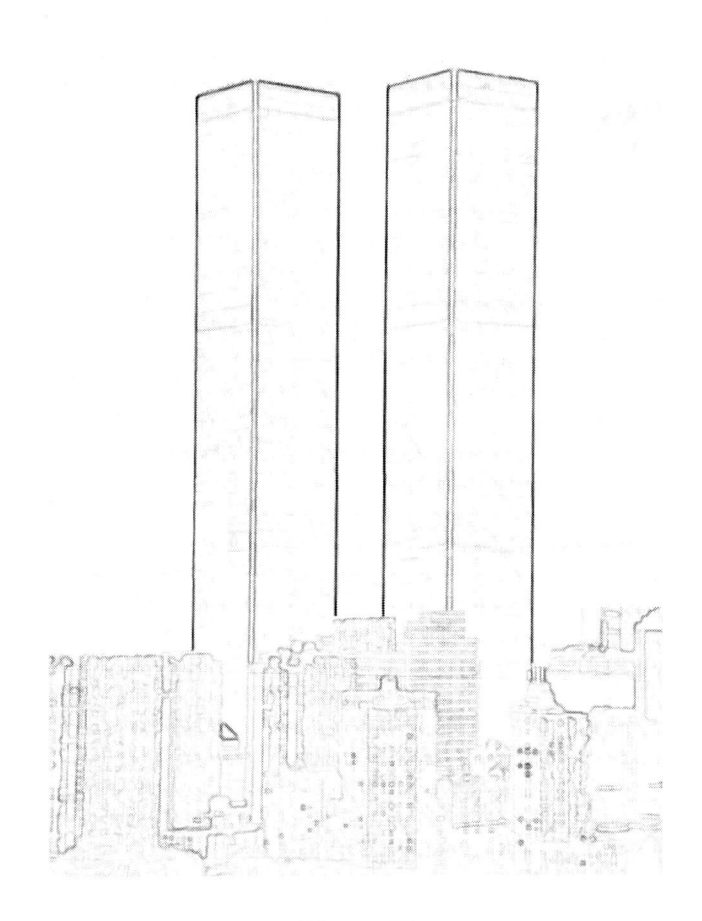

Figure 23

Two high-rise buildings with a narrow gap, the shape is like one building cut into two by an axe from the sky.

73

Section III – Interior Feng Shui

Feng Shui divides spaces into 'Universes' for studying purposes. For example, the whole city is a big Universe, the neighbourhood is a medium Universe and your home is a small Universe. You can go one step further to define that a room is a tiny Universe and apply theories to that room only.

A Universe is, in fact, the particular space that we apply Feng Shui theories on it. The exterior of a home is a Universe and the interior of it is another Universe. After studying the exterior of your home, we can now go to study the interior of your home; which is a smaller Universe.

While the exterior environment of your home sets up the basic framework of your Feng Shui, the interior also affects you in many ways and the effects are considerably heavy.

Aquarium

Having an aquarium at home is a good idea, as it brings life to the family and Water means Wealth in Feng Shui. However, the location of the aquarium may create a problem. For example, you should not place an aquarium in a spot that belongs to Fire, as Water and Fire are not compatible in nature.

It is difficult to tell which spot in your home belongs to Fire without knowing the basic principles of Bagua. However, you should not place an aquarium in the kitchen and you should not place it inside your bedroom either.

A kitchen is Fire in nature while an aquarium is Water in nature. As a result, putting an aquarium in the kitchen is like adding water to a fire. Water is not good in the bedroom, as water represents movement and bedrooms are supposed to be stable for rest. Water beds are therefore not good in Feng Shui as they 'vibrate' too much.

The water level of your aquarium is also an issue that you have to take care of. If there is no chair or sofa beside the aquarium, you should measure the water level as you stand. If there is a sofa or chair beside the aquarium, then you should measure the water level as you sit on that sofa. The rule is that the water level should not be higher than your nose when you stand or sit respectively.

Bad Odour

Bad odours inside your home are annoying. As discussed in the Exterior Feng Shui, bad odours are bad Qi and should be eliminated.

Bad odours in homes may come from rotten foods, faded plants or dirty water in vases. You can eliminate those odours by simply cleaning up your refrigerator and vases.

Artificial scents are not suggested to be used to cover the bad odours, as the artificial scents are chemicals and thus are not a good source of Qi. However, natural scents from fresh fruits and flowers are good ways to bring freshness to your home.

There are some bad odours that may exist without getting noticed. For example, there may be bad odours coming from your sinks or other sewer pipes and you may not notice them unless you pay close attention to them.

There is a U-shaped trap under the sink that keeps the gases from the sewer line from being able to come back inside your house. The trap works because water sits in that U-shaped section of pipe, and therefore the bad odour (the gases) cannot get back up through the drain. This kind of U-shaped trap is installed in every drain to make sure that the gases from sewer system cannot get back.

If you do not use a sink for a while, or the drain in your basement has dried out; bad odours may come from those drains. You can simply add water to the drains and the water will block the smell.

On the other hand, bacteria may grow inside those U-traps and generate bad odours. Many companies claim their cleansers may eliminates those odours, but the most effective way is to pour a pot of boiling water into the drain to kill the bacteria.

Bad smell is a Sha and is Yin in nature. If you cannot totally eliminate it, you can keep a light on in that area all the time to lower its Yin.

Beams

Beams (Figure 24) on the ceiling are not good Feng Shui, they represent pressure and burden on you.

You should never sleep or sit directly under a beam, as it presses on you and will make you tire and hinder your luck.

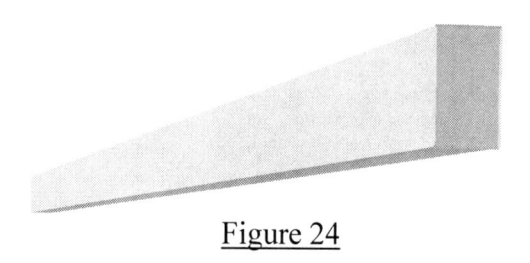

Figure 24

A beam represents pressure and burden.

You should move your bed or seat to a position that is not directly under any beam. If it is your office and your space is assigned so that you cannot move to another location, you can put a plant with strong stem beside or on your table as a support to the beam. To name a few, pachira macrocarpa, bamboos, dracaena deremensis and any bonsai are all good plants for this purpose.

Bed

On average we spend eight hours in our beds and thus the bedroom is one the most important places in residential Feng Shui.

It is important to know where the best spot to put your bed is. Your bed should be placed according to your own trigram. You can use the appendices at the back to find out your own trigram and the corresponding favour directions to select the one suitable for your bedroom. Moreover, there are some basic rules to follow on how you put your bed.

First of all, you should put your bed with the head against a wall to give it support (Figure 25). While other settings are acceptable, you should not put your bed in the middle of your bedroom and should have only one side of your bed touch a wall.

Every bed should have a headboard, as headboards are the support of beds.

Without a headboard for your bed, you will have no support in your daily life.

If your bed is backing onto a wall with window above it, you should keep the window blinds closed at all times. A bigger headboard is also needed in order to provide a stronger support to the bed as the window weakens the original support given by the wall.

Good

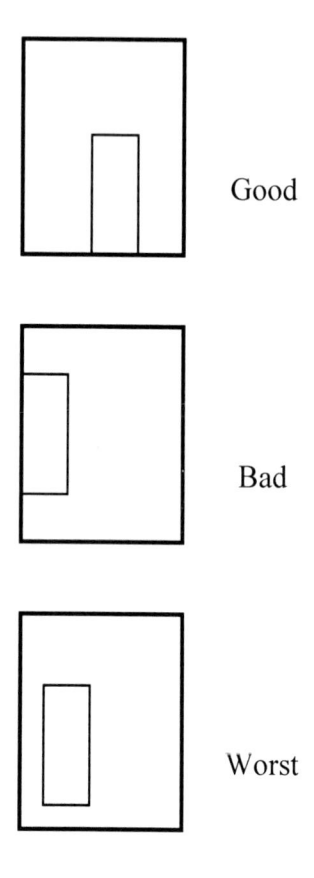

Bad

Worst

<u>Figure 25</u>

Bed should be put with its head against a wall

Bedroom Light

It is more convenient to have a ceiling light in our bedroom, but a floor light or table light is better in Feng Shui.

Having a light in the bedroom ceiling is like having something above you press on you when you sleep. If possible, it is better to use floor lights, table lights or wall lights. If a ceiling light must be used, you should pay attention to the shape of the light.

The bedroom is a place for rest so the light should be stable in nature. Therefore, bedroom ceiling lights should be square or rectangular in shape, as such shapes represent stability.

A more important point about ceiling light fixtures is that there should be no sharp point coming from the shed or the frame. Any sharp tip pointing to your bed is not good and should be avoided.

Centre of a Home

When we apply the Bagua theory to a home, the middle of the home is left unassigned to any kind of luck (Figure 26). Actually, the centre of a home is like the heart of the body; the Qi passes through the centre and go to other rooms, so it should not be blocked or occupied.

Since the centre is used to store and direct Qi, it means the Qi of a home will sit on the centre and will stay there even when the home has a new owner (a major renovation can change this fact). Replacing the centre of a house will give the house a new heart, which will give new Qi to it.

If you know something bad has happened to the previous owner or the house is very old (say, more than 60 years old), then you may want to change the centre of it by replacing the tiles or hardwood floors in that area. This may change the luck of the house.

If possible, you can also dig the ground and change the soil under it and open the ceiling (such as installing a skylight) at the same time. Opening the ceiling is the traditional way to change the luck of a house, from a Period to another Period (20 years of time, 2004 – 2023 is Period 8).

Wealth	Fame & Reputation	Love & Marriage
Health & Family	**Centre**	Children & Creativity
Knowledge & Wisdom	Career	Helps & Friends

Figure 26

In Feng Shui, a home is divided into nine parts in order to know how to boost the different kind of luck; the centre is not assigned for anything.

Chandelier

A chandelier is similar to a beam, which presses on you. Chandeliers also have sharp tips, which are not good.

If the chandelier is in the dining room, you should put a dining table under the chandelier for support even if that dinning room is not used. One more benefit of it is to prevent people from hurting their heads when passing through that room as the dining chandelier is usually hung at a lower position than a chandelier in a hallway or foyer area.

If the chandelier is in the family room or living room, you should place a coffee table under it.

In all cases, you should not place any sofa under it and should not sit right under any chandelier.

The foyer is the best location for a chandelier as you will not stay in the foyer for a long period of time so the effect will not be long and will not be significant.

You should place a table under a chandelier whenever it is possible as a support to the chandelier. Apart from Feng Shui, the table can also block people from staying right under the chandelier and keep them safe in case the chandelier falls.

Choice of Colours

The colours of your walls are important, so are the colours of other things such as furniture, carpets, and appliances.

The five elements have their own colours to represent them. Red represents Fire, yellow represents Earth, white represents Metal, black represents Water and green represents Wood.

If you want to boost up an element, for example, Earth in a room; you can consider using yellow or red as the colour of the wall paint, carpet or furniture. Using the colour yellow or green can also control Water in that room.

However, you should not paint your bedroom black even if you want to boost the Water in that bedroom. As discussed in the above paragraphs regarding aquariums, water is not suitable in a bedroom and neither is black. A room painted in black is in fact not suitable for sleep, study and work (except for a dark room).

The general colour requirements for rooms are light colours for the ceiling and dark colours for the floor.

Corner with Windows

Large windows may be good for letting sunlight in the building, but a corner with windows on both sides (Figure 27) creates a very bad Sha and should be avoided.

People sitting or sleeping at such locations will receive the heavy Sha everyday and the consequence can be very serious. This kind of construction is very common in office buildings and you should avoid sitting at such a location.

When sitting or sleeping at a corner like this, you must keep the blinds of one of the windows closed to make it look like just a single sided window.

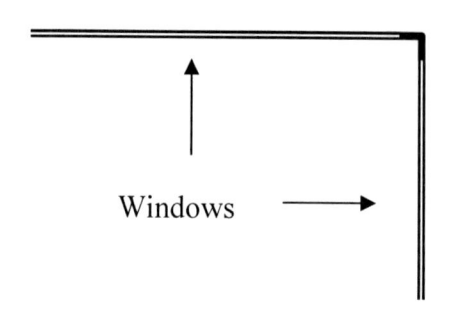

Figure 27

A corner with windows on both sides is not good at all.

Corners and Sharp Edges

There are columns, air ducts and furniture that may have corners or sharp edges. These edges are not good in Feng Shui as they are Sha pointing to you (Figure 28).

Round tables are better than rectangular or square ones as round tables have no corners. Similarly, round columns are better than square ones and so on.

If your bed or seat is facing such a sharp edge, you can place a piece of jade between the edge and your bed (or seat) to eliminate the Sha.

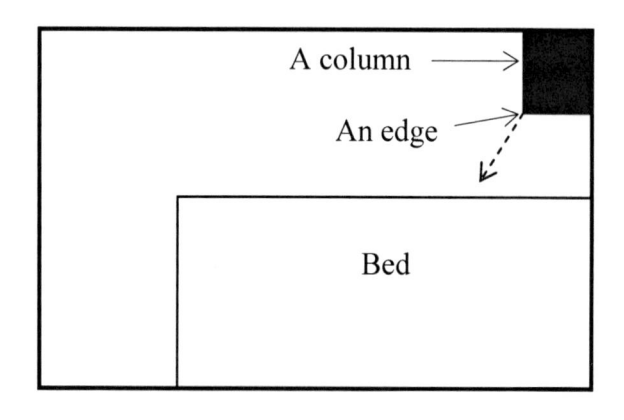

Figure 28

An edge pointing to a bed

Damp Bathroom

Most bathrooms are damp as water evaporates from the toilets and sinks. Since both bathroom and water are Yin in nature; therefore, a damp bathroom is too Yin and should be improved.

The first thing to do is to keep your bathroom clean. It is because if there are moistures in the bathroom, you will want it to be clean moistures.

An exhaust fan should be installed and used to take the moisture away. The bathroom door should always be closed to prevent the Yin coming out from it.

If the bathroom is bright enough, a foliage plant can be placed in it to absorb the Yin. However, if there is not enough sunlight in the room, the dying plant will increase the Yin on the contrary.

The Entrance Door

The entrance is the mouth of your home and is one of the most important parts. Entrances should not be blocked as the Qi (wealth) has to enter our homes freely from the outside through the entrances.

The colour of your entrance door should match with your trigram, which can be found in the Appendices at the back.

You may use a black and white wavy carpet in the entrance so that it can lead the wealth into your home. It is because the colour black and wavy shapes both represent Water, and Water represents wealth. The white colour represents Metal, which supports Water.

For apartment units, it is not uncommon that the entrance door is directly opposite to a bedroom door or a bathroom door (Figure 29). If this happens, you should place a table or any large piece of furniture in between the two doors. The bathroom door or bedroom door should always be closed.

If your entrance door is directly facing a window; you should block the view by closing the window blinds or placing some plants on that window sill.

Similarly, an entrance door should not be in line with a back door, such as a patio door. In such a case, you should block the space by installing an extra door or placing a large piece of furniture in between.

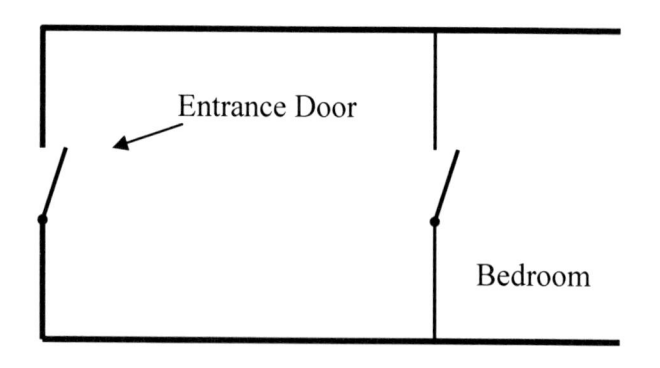

Figure 29

Entrance door is inline with a bedroom door.

Flowers

Flowers are good for homes as they are beautiful and bring fragrance to us. There are, however, some guidelines on having flowers at home.

You should never put flowers or plants in the bedroom, as a bedroom is Yin and flowers and plants are Yang. Having flowers in the bedroom will bring undesirable love and affairs, which will jeopardize the spousal relationship.

Flowers in pots are the best as they are living plants and represent life. Freshly cut flowers are good but they should be replaced or discarded once they have wilted.

Dry flowers are not good in Feng Shui; they present failures and loss of life. Dry flowers are in fact the dead bodies of plants and they will become dusty over time with particles coming out from their bodies, so they are not good to both your health and luck.

Plastic flowers are good substitutes for dry flowers as they are not dead bodies and will not, normally, release any waste.

Folding Doors and Gates

Folding doors and sliding metal gates are more common in modern cities as metal gates provide more security and folding doors can save space (Figure 30).

Since sliding and folding doors cannot be fully opened and part of them will block the entrance, they will block the Qi from entering your home and from circulating the Qi into your rooms. Therefore, you should avoid using them if possible.

Similarly, you should keep the doorways clear in all your bedrooms, bathrooms and other rooms.

All doors should be functioning well and not be blocked so that they are able to be opened fully to let the Qi circulate.

Sliding Metal Gate

Folding Door

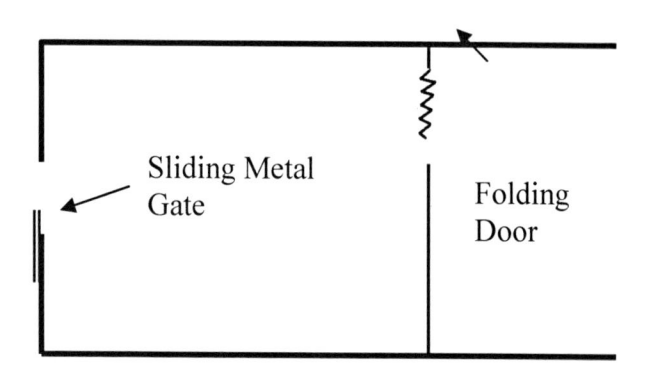

Figure 30

The sliding gate and folding door will block Qi.

Main Entrance Facing the Stairway

It is quite common in North America to have the main entrance of a house directly face the stairway.

More and more people now know this setting is a bad Feng Shui as the Wealth of your home will slide from the stairs to the outside through the main entrance.

If there is a door sill in the main entrance that is three inches or higher, then it will help you to prevent the wealth from escaping by blocking it on the ground.

If your home has no door sill or it is less than three inches high; then you should place a concave mirror above the door, facing the inside, to absorb the Wealth so that it will not run away from your home.

House is too Large

It is good to have a big house, even a mansion. However, it may not be a good Feng Shui if the house is too large.

The Yin and Yang has to be balanced in a home and the Qi has to be circulated among rooms. When a house is too large, there are not enough people to balance the Yin and Yang and not enough people to stir the Qi among rooms.

How can you know that a house is too large for you? It is quite subjective sometimes, as we have to consider the number of people living in the house, the setting of the house and the layout of it. Basically, the average useable area in a house per person should not be more than five hundred square feet, excluding the foyer, stairs, hallways and other open areas.

The other way to calculate is that one thousand square feet should be assigned to the foyer, stairs, hallways and other open areas, every person can have five hundred square feet to use. That is, one person can occupy up to one thousand and five hundred square feet; two persons can occupy up to two thousand square feet; three persons can occupy up to two thousand five hundred square feet and so on.

Many people like to have a big master bedroom too. The same rule applies to bedrooms – they should not be too large. If a house or a room is too large, you can place big furniture in it to make it feel more 'solid'. You may also invite friends to visit you more often to give the house more Yang.

Kitchen and Bathroom

No one is willing to eat in a bathroom. These two rooms are contradictory in nature, thus they are normally separated by a distance. However, it is possible to have a kitchen next or opposite to a bathroom in some small homes.

It is not good to have a kitchen next to a bathroom. If that happens, you should always keep both doors closed and place a tall and slim plant in between (Figure 31).

If the kitchen door is directly opposite to a bathroom door, you should put a screen or a curtain in between them to prevent the Qi from exchanging between the two rooms.

Bathroom Kitchen

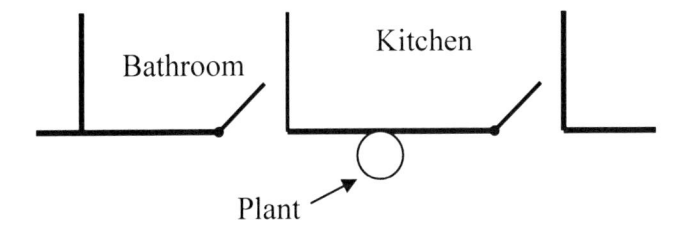

Plant

Figure 31

Put a plant between the doors of kitchen and bathroom.

Marble Floor

Marble tiles are the 'standard' floorings for million dollar homes. Marble was extensively used for sculptures and as a building material in many countries. You can find it in many churches, temples and monuments.

In ancient China and some other countries, marble was used only in mausoleums and tombs. To be exact, marble was used for only Yin (the deceased) residence. Therefore, marble is not suitable for use in our homes as it is too Yin to have it.

You may have a small portion of home that is made with marble, such as a marble window sill or marble countertop. However, a marble floor or a marble wall is too Yin and should be avoided.

If you already have a marble floor, you can put some rugs and runners on it to cover it. The rugs can 'warm up' the cold marble surface so that the Yin can be lowered. On the other hand, the choice of colours (Appendix D) of the rugs can help you boost one Element when needed.

Mirrors

Mirrors in Feng Shui are tools. We have convex mirrors, flat mirrors and concave mirrors to be used for different purposes.

Mirrors are used to collect, divert or reflect Qi, both good and bad. Placing a mirror at home without knowing its function and the nature of the spot is dangerous, as the mirror may disturb the Qi, attract or reflect bad Qi to you.

In general, all mirrors should be covered at home and should only be uncovered when they are used. The only exception may be in the bathroom, as bathroom is the place where we will stay the least time and it is more convenient for modern people to have big mirrors fixed in their bathrooms. However, a wall to wall mirror is too big and should be avoided.

Dressing mirrors should be installed inside cabinets or closets so that they will not be seen when the cabinets and closets are closed.

You should never place a mirror in a bedroom facing your bed. It will disturb your Qi and your sleep too. It will also affect your luck. Placing a mirror to face a door is also not recommended.

Similarly, television and computer monitors should also not be placed in bedrooms. If you want to, they should be covered or placed in a cabinet with a door.

Missing Corner(s)

The best shape of a house or an apartment unit is a square. The worst type is an irregular shape with the four missing corners of a square or a round one without corners.

A home with one or more missing corners (Figure 32) represents its lack of some luck and the resident in the corresponding Bagua position will have problems (Figure 33).

For example, a house with a missing corner at the west means the eldest son will have bad luck. If the family has no son, it will mean the couple will not have son but daughters.

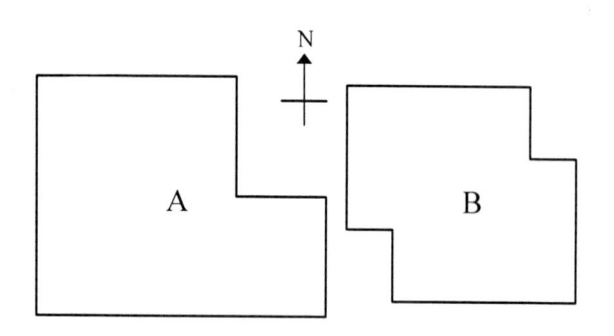

Figure 32

House A is missing the North East corner and House B is missing the North East and South West corners.

North West Eldest Daughter	North Middle Daughter	North East Mother
West Eldest Son		East Youngest Daughter
South West Youngest Son	South Middle Son	South East Father

Figure 33

Each direction in Bagua represents a person at home.

Nails and Hanging Hooks

We put nails and hooks on walls and ceilings to hang frames, flower pots or other stuff. When they are not used, you should take them out to make the wall (ceilings) flat.

As we have discussed before, having a sharp edge pointing to you is not good. Nails and hooks without anything to be hung on are sharp objects, just like knives on the wall, pointing to you everyday.

If you let those nails and hooks stay on walls without covering them (hanging something on them), they will create bad Qi and point to you.

You should take out the nail or hook whenever you don't need it.

Office Desk and Chair

The best setting of your desk and chair is that the office desk is facing an open space and your chair is backing onto a wall (Figure 34).

If your desk is facing against a wall, it will give you pressure with a bad flow of Qi (Figure 35). To solve this problem, you can place a small plant on your desk. Four bamboos in a vase is one of the best choices.

If your chair is not backing onto a wall, it will make you have no support from your boss or other colleagues. The solution is to use a high back chair and put a dark yellow coat or jacket on the back to use as a support for you.

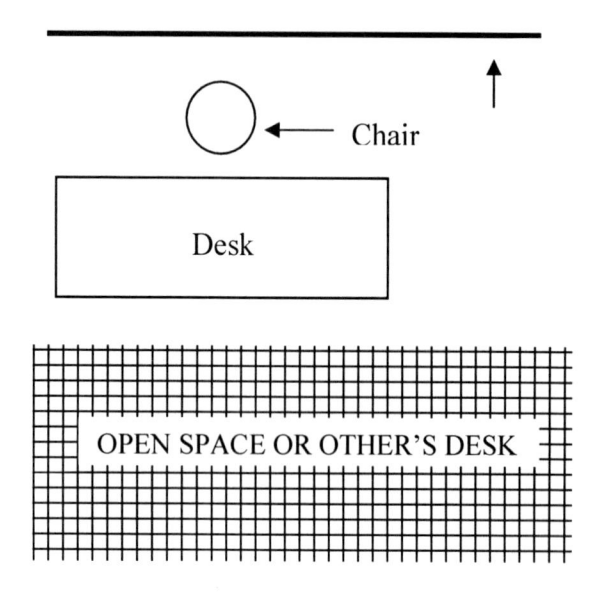

Figure 34

Your desk should not be facing a wall, and your chair should be backing onto a wall.

```
┌─────────────────────────────────────┐
│   OPEN SPACE OR OTHER'S DESK        │
└─────────────────────────────────────┘
```

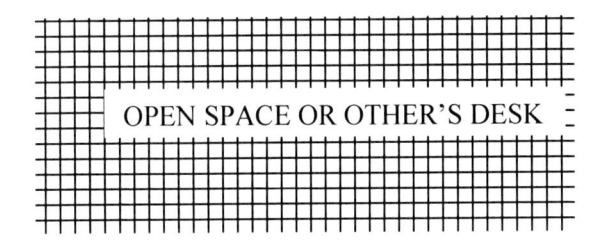

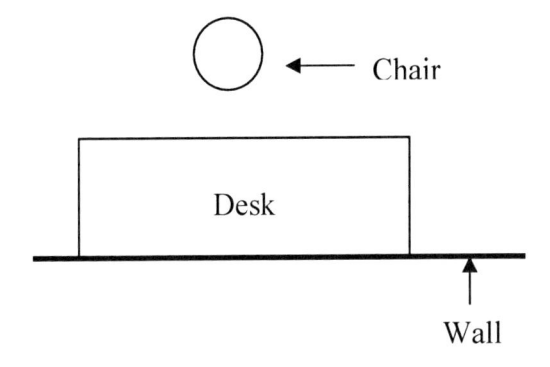

◯ ← Chair

Desk

↑
Wall

Figure 35

A desk faces a wall is not good and your chair should not be backing onto other people's desk or open space.

Plants

Not every room is suitable for placing plants. For example, kitchens and bedrooms are not suitable to have any plants. Since plants belong to the Wood element, they should be placed in rooms that need Wood to balance the other elements or to boost the Wood element in that room.

Plants should be green and healthy. Fading plants represent failing and should be trimmed or replaced. Begonias, geraniums, ivy and spider plant all are beautiful plants, but they are not good plants for Feng Shui purposes.

Plants give support to a home and represent growth and prosperity. Therefore, hanging plants are not good in Feng Shui because they are too soft to support themselves; they spill over the edge of the basket and grow downwards.

Posters, Statues and Ornaments

Unlike offices and other workplaces, our home is the place we rest and thus should be calm in nature.

Posters and statues with armies, fighters, vampires and all other scary or violent themes are not suitable at home. They will make the residents hot-tempered or even violent.

Nude posters and statues are not suitable either, as they will spoil the spousal relationship. If the occupant is single, they will make it impossible for the occupant to find a companion.

Some people like paintings of wild animals such as tigers, wolves or lions. These animals are offensive in nature, so they are not recommended for homes. If you really want to hang such kind of paintings at home, you should pay attention to the position of the animals. They should be facing the outside or on the ground (you will see their backs instead of their faces) so that they will not be able to attack you.

Ornaments such as knives, guns and deer head mounts are not suitable for homes. They are too Yang and may bring violence to your home. You should remove all these kinds of ornaments to calm down your home. However, if you belong to the Yang professions such as the police force, army or butcher, this kind of ornament may increase your Yang so that you can do your job better. However, they may still be harmful to other family members. You should put such ornament in your workplace instead of your home, unless you live alone.

Rectangular Shape Room

Most of our rooms are rectangle in shape. The ratio of width and length of a rectangular room should not be higher than 2:1.

A long room is not good and may bring bad luck as its shape is similar to a coffin. To change its coffin shape, you can divide the room into two by placing cabinets or other large furniture in the middle of the room (Figure 36).

However, you should not divide a bedroom that is occupied by a couple. Dividing a room will also divide the relationship of the people sharing the same room. Therefore, it is not recommended to do that in bedrooms.

[A cabinet or a three sided fireplace.]

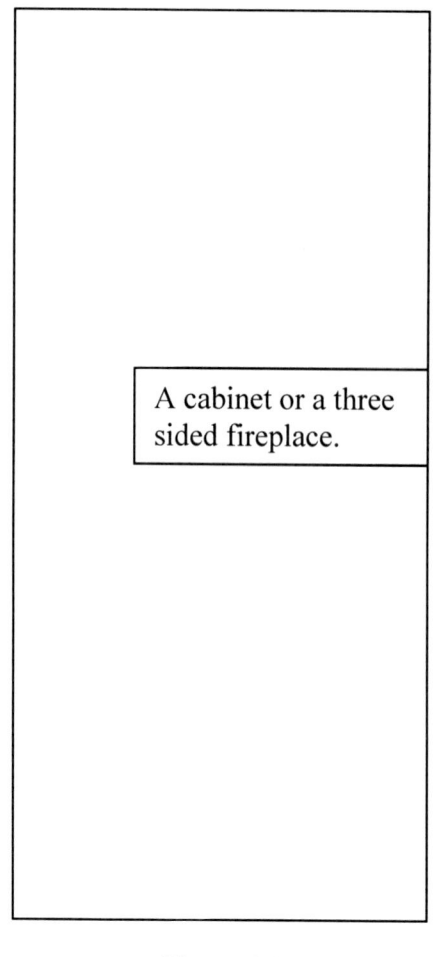

Figure 36

Dividing a room by a piece of furniture.

Stairs

Stairs provide us access from one floor to another floor. It also provides a pathway for Qi. Therefore, stairs are very important in Feng Shui.

It is not good to have a circular stairway, because it is too curved that it will stir up all the Qi in your house and make you restless.

Stair should not be in the centre of a house, as its stirring force is the strongest. Just imagine when you stir a glass of water; the centre is always the most vigorous. Having a circular stair in the centre of a house is the worst.

To slow down the circulation of Qi generated by a circular stairway, you can place a plant at the end of the stairs to block the Qi. This is particularly useful and important for two circular stairs on different levels that are connected together.

The Scarlett O'Hara stair is elegant but, again, elegant items may not good in Feng Shui.

The design of the Scarlett O'Hara stair is a Y shaped stairway with a wide section at the bottom and splitting at the middle, going to two opposite directions above.

This kind of design is in fact splitting the family members into to two different directions. It will make the people living there have a sense of separation and eventually a lack of communications.

All types of stairs that split at the end have the same kind of effect on the residents. If possible, you should block one side of the stairs.

Stove

The direction of your stove is very important. It should not be facing the back of your house (Figure 37). That is, when you cook, you should not be facing the front of your house. You should move the stove to the other three directions.

The stove should not be placed next to the sink, as the water faucet belongs to the element Water and the stove belongs to the element Fire. Water and Fire cannot be put together. If you cannot relocate them, you can place a metal barrier or stone (such as marble) barrier between them to separate the Water and Fire.

The stove should not be directly exposed to sunlight. You should close the blind to prevent sunlight from shining directly on the stove.

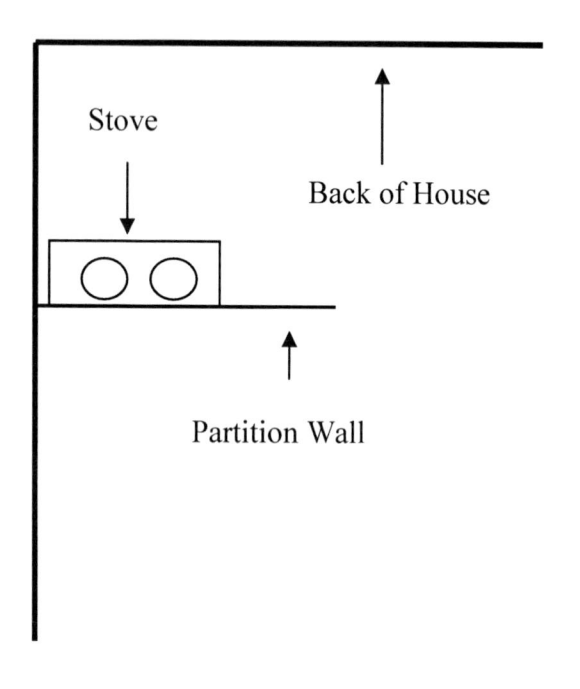

Figure 37

The stove is 'facing' the back of the house, which is not good.

Swimming Pool

In North America, many house owners like to have a swimming pool in their backyard. Having a pool in the backyard is a bad Feng Shui, because we need a solid ground (preferable some trees) as a support at our back. A swimming pool is a hollow ground and gives no support to the house.

Just imagine it is just like you are working on something outdoors, and there is a pool behind you; you are 'trapped' and can easily fall into the pool. It is therefore not recommended to have a pool in the backyard.

A Swimming pool should be kidney shaped or in the shape of a figure '8', as they represent luck and wealth. Having a rectangular shaped swimming pool is the worst. You should decorate it, using wavy pattern tiles, to make it look like a curved shape other than a rectangle.

Two Entrance Doors

Some homes have two entrance doors, especially those that are combined units. Some people like to buy two adjacent semi-detached houses and make it a large detached home. All these homes with two entrance doors will have the effect of separation.

Like the Scarlett O'Hara stairway, a home with two entrance doors will split the family members into two different directions. It will make the people living there have a sense of separation and eventually a lack of communications. The relationships among them will be spoiled.

You should block or lock one of the doors and use only the other one.

Appendix A – Trigram Table

Birth Year*	Male	Female
1901	9	6
1902	8	7
1903	7	8
1904	6	9
1905	5	1
1906	4	2
1907	3	3
1908	2	4
1909	1	5
1910	9	6
1911	8	7
1912	7	8
1913	6	9
1914	5	1
1915	4	2
1916	3	3
1917	2	4
1918	1	5
1919	9	6
1920	8	7
1921	7	8
1922	6	9
1923	5	1
1924	4	2
1925	3	3
1926	2	4
1927	1	5
1928	9	6
1929	8	7
1930	7	8

Birth Year*	Male	Female
1931	6	9
1932	5	1
1933	4	2
1934	3	3
1935	2	4
1936	1	5
1937	9	6
1938	8	7
1939	7	8
1940	6	9
1941	5	1
1942	4	2
1943	3	3
1944	2	4
1945	1	5
1946	9	6
1947	8	7
1948	7	8
1949	6	9
1950	5	1
1951	4	2
1952	3	3
1953	2	4
1954	1	5
1955	9	6
1956	8	7
1957	7	8
1958	6	9
1959	5	1
1960	4	2

Birth Year*	Male	Female
1961	3	3
1962	2	4
1963	1	5
1964	9	6
1965	8	7
1966	7	8
1967	6	9
1968	5	1
1969	4	2
1970	3	3
1971	2	4
1972	1	5
1973	9	6
1974	8	7
1975	7	8
1976	6	9
1977	5	1
1978	4	2
1979	3	3
1980	2	4
1981	1	5
1982	9	6
1983	8	7
1984	7	8
1985	6	9
1986	5	1
1987	4	2
1988	3	3
1989	2	4
1990	1	5

Birth Year*	Male	Female
1991	9	6
1992	8	7
1993	7	8
1994	6	9
1995	5	1
1996	4	2
1997	3	3
1998	2	4
1999	1	5
2000	9	6
2001	8	7
2002	7	8
2003	6	9
2004	5	1
2005	4	2
2006	3	3
2007	2	4
2008	1	5
2009	9	6
2010	8	7
2011	7	8
2012	6	9
2013	5	1
2014	4	2
2015	3	3
2016	2	4
2017	1	5
2018	9	6
2019	8	7
2020	7	8

* If your birthday is between Jan 1 and Feb 3 (inclusive), you have to use the year before as your birth year.

Appendix B
Trigram and Element

Trigram	Element
1	Water
2	Earth
3	Wood
4	Wood
5	Earth
6	Metal
7	Metal
8	Earth
9	Fire

Appendix C
Elements and Directions

Element	Favourable Directions
Water	North, West, North-west
Wood	East, South-east, North
Fire	South, East, South-east
Earth	South, South-west, North-east
Metal	West, North-west, South-west, North-east

Appendix D
Elements and Colours

Element	Favourable Colours
Water	Black, White
Wood	Green, Black
Fire	Red, Green
Earth	Yellow, Red
Metal	White, Yellow

Appendix E
Favourable Professions

The favourable professions for each trigram:

1	Philosophy, religion, economics, archaeology, insurance, banking, diplomats, research, restaurants, bars, café, textile dyeing, petroleum, paints, printing, subway, real estate, night shift work, day care, kindergarten, elementary school teacher, children books, toys, fire fighter.
2	Civil engineering, real estate, agriculture, obstetrics and gynaecology, nanny, dietician, arts & crafts, antiques, textile manufacturing, tailor, china and ceramic, teacher, service industry, cat and cow breeder.
3	Media, orchestra, vocalist, musical instruments, singer, receptionist, interpreter, telecommunication, music, recording, editing, performer, literature, gardening, bee farm, pet shop, horse barn.
4	Cosmetics, beauty salon, hair stylist, advertising, interior design, gardening, herbs, fragrance, paper, stationeries, books, literature, art, sales, aero equipment, airlines, chicken farm.

5	Politician, judge, management, control centre, funeral home, memorial service, land related industries, fine art, musician, recycling, antique, pathology.
6	Public servants, legal, politician, security, astronomy, aero space, nuclear energy, computer, petroleum, mining, metal manufacturing, glass, gem, stock exchange, insurance, actuary, precision equipment, mass transportation, automotive, gym, race course, zoo, circus, martial arts, consultant.
7	Lawyer, legal consultant, public relation, finance, banking, sales, editor, interpretation, public speaker, surgeon, dentist, hardware, dollar store, artists, café, feminine products, aquaria products, pet shop, columnist.
8	Hotel, department store, real estate, banking, supermarket, religion, leather, water proofing products, meat shop, agency, trainer, mining, property management, jewelry, cement and stone.
9	Scholar, teacher, army, psychologist, model, television, electronic, chemistry, firearm, medial lab, detective, pilot, religion, art, diplomat, natural resources, solar energy, obstetrics and gynaecology.

LaVergne, TN USA
16 September 2010
197198LV00004B/1/P